Action Planner

Belong To:

_____

Action Priority Matrix

TASK #	PRIORITY LIST	DUE DATE	DONE
			☐
			☐
			☐
			☐
			☐
			☐
			☐
			☐
			☐

IMPACT

QUICK *Wins* ● ● ●

MAJOR *Projects* ● ● ●

FILL-IN *Jobs* ● ● ●

THANKLESS *Tasks* ● ● ●

EFFORT

Notes

Action Priority Matrix

TASK #	PRIORITY LIST	DUE DATE	DONE
			☐
			☐
			☐
			☐
			☐
			☐
			☐
			☐
			☐
			☐

IMPACT

QUICK *Wins* ● ● ●	MAJOR *Projects* ● ● ●
FILL-IN *Jobs* ● ● ●	THANKLESS *Tasks* ● ● ●

EFFORT

Notes

Action Priority Matrix

TASK #	PRIORITY LIST	DUE DATE	DONE
			☐
			☐
			☐
			☐
			☐
			☐
			☐
			☐
			☐

IMPACT

QUICK *Wins* ● ● ●

MAJOR *Projects* ● ● ●

FILL-IN *Jobs* ● ● ●

THANKLESS *Tasks* ● ● ●

EFFORT

Notes

Action Priority Matrix

TASK #	PRIORITY LIST	DUE DATE	DONE
			☐
			☐
			☐
			☐
			☐
			☐
			☐
			☐
			☐

IMPACT

QUICK *Wins* ● ● ●

MAJOR *Projects* ● ● ●

FILL-IN *Jobs* ● ● ●

THANKLESS *Tasks* ● ● ●

EFFORT

Notes

Action Priority Matrix

TASK #	PRIORITY LIST	DUE DATE	DONE
			☐
			☐
			☐
			☐
			☐
			☐
			☐
			☐
			☐

IMPACT

QUICK *Wins* ● ● ●

MAJOR *Projects* ● ● ●

FILL-IN *Jobs* ● ● ●

THANKLESS *Tasks* ● ● ●

EFFORT

Notes

Action Priority Matrix

TASK #	PRIORITY LIST	DUE DATE	DONE
			☐
			☐
			☐
			☐
			☐
			☐
			☐
			☐
			☐

IMPACT

QUICK *Wins* ● ● ●	MAJOR *Projects* ● ● ●
FILL-IN *Jobs* ● ● ●	THANKLESS *Tasks* ● ● ●

EFFORT

Notes

Action Priority Matrix

TASK #	PRIORITY LIST	DUE DATE	DONE
			☐
			☐
			☐
			☐
			☐
			☐
			☐
			☐
			☐

IMPACT

QUICK *Wins* ● ● ●

MAJOR *Projects* ● ● ●

FILL-IN *Jobs* ● ● ●

THANKLESS *Tasks* ● ● ●

EFFORT

Notes

Action Priority Matrix

TASK #	PRIORITY LIST	DUE DATE	DONE
			☐
			☐
			☐
			☐
			☐
			☐
			☐
			☐
			☐

IMPACT

QUICK *Wins* ● ● ●

MAJOR *Projects* ● ● ●

FILL-IN *Jobs* ● ● ●

THANKLESS *Tasks* ● ● ●

EFFORT

Notes

Action Priority Matrix

TASK #	PRIORITY LIST	DUE DATE	DONE
			☐
			☐
			☐
			☐
			☐
			☐
			☐
			☐
			☐

QUICK *Wins* ● ● ●

MAJOR *Projects* ● ● ●

FILL-IN *Jobs* ● ● ●

THANKLESS *Tasks* ● ● ●

IMPACT

EFFORT

Notes

Action Priority Matrix

TASK #	PRIORITY LIST	DUE DATE	DONE
			☐
			☐
			☐
			☐
			☐
			☐
			☐
			☐
			☐

IMPACT

QUICK *Wins* ● ● ●	MAJOR *Projects* ● ● ●
FILL-IN *Jobs* ● ● ●	THANKLESS *Tasks* ● ● ●

EFFORT

Notes

Action Priority Matrix

TASK #	PRIORITY LIST	DUE DATE	DONE
			☐
			☐
			☐
			☐
			☐
			☐
			☐
			☐
			☐
			☐

IMPACT

QUICK *Wins* ● ● ●

MAJOR *Projects* ● ● ●

FILL-IN *Jobs* ● ● ●

THANKLESS *Tasks* ● ● ●

EFFORT

Notes

Action Priority Matrix

TASK #	PRIORITY LIST	DUE DATE	DONE
			☐
			☐
			☐
			☐
			☐
			☐
			☐
			☐
			☐

IMPACT

QUICK *Wins* ● ● ●

MAJOR *Projects* ● ● ●

FILL-IN *Jobs* ● ● ●

THANKLESS *Tasks* ● ● ●

EFFORT

Notes

Action Priority Matrix

TASK #	PRIORITY LIST	DUE DATE	DONE
			☐
			☐
			☐
			☐
			☐
			☐
			☐
			☐
			☐

IMPACT

QUICK *Wins* ● ● ●

MAJOR *Projects* ● ● ●

FILL-IN *Jobs* ● ● ●

THANKLESS *Tasks* ● ● ●

EFFORT

Notes

Action Priority Matrix

TASK #	PRIORITY LIST	DUE DATE	DONE
			☐
			☐
			☐
			☐
			☐
			☐
			☐
			☐
			☐

IMPACT

QUICK *Wins* ● ● ●	MAJOR *Projects* ● ● ●
FILL-IN *Jobs* ● ● ●	THANKLESS *Tasks* ● ● ●

EFFORT

Notes

Action Priority Matrix

TASK #	PRIORITY LIST	DUE DATE	DONE
			☐
			☐
			☐
			☐
			☐
			☐
			☐
			☐
			☐

IMPACT

QUICK *Wins* ● ● ●

MAJOR *Projects* ● ● ●

FILL-IN *Jobs* ● ● ●

THANKLESS *Tasks* ● ● ●

EFFORT

Notes

Action Priority Matrix

TASK #	PRIORITY LIST	DUE DATE	DONE
			☐
			☐
			☐
			☐
			☐
			☐
			☐
			☐
			☐

IMPACT

QUICK *Wins* ● ● ●

MAJOR *Projects* ● ● ●

FILL-IN *Jobs* ● ● ●

THANKLESS *Tasks* ● ● ●

EFFORT

Notes

Action Priority Matrix

TASK #	PRIORITY LIST	DUE DATE	DONE
			☐
			☐
			☐
			☐
			☐
			☐
			☐
			☐
			☐

IMPACT

QUICK *Wins* ● ● ●

MAJOR *Projects* ● ● ●

FILL-IN *Jobs* ● ● ●

THANKLESS *Tasks* ● ● ●

EFFORT

Notes

Action Priority Matrix

TASK #	PRIORITY LIST	DUE DATE	DONE
			☐
			☐
			☐
			☐
			☐
			☐
			☐
			☐
			☐

IMPACT

QUICK *Wins* ● ● ●

MAJOR *Projects* ● ● ●

FILL-IN *Jobs* ● ● ●

THANKLESS *Tasks* ● ● ●

EFFORT

Notes

Action Priority Matrix

TASK #	PRIORITY LIST	DUE DATE	DONE
			☐
			☐
			☐
			☐
			☐
			☐
			☐
			☐
			☐

IMPACT

QUICK *Wins* ● ● ●

MAJOR *Projects* ● ● ●

FILL-IN *Jobs* ● ● ●

THANKLESS *Tasks* ● ● ●

EFFORT

Notes

Action Priority Matrix

TASK #	PRIORITY LIST	DUE DATE	DONE
			☐
			☐
			☐
			☐
			☐
			☐
			☐
			☐
			☐

IMPACT →

QUICK *Wins* ● ● ●	MAJOR *Projects* ● ● ●
FILL-IN *Jobs* ● ● ●	THANKLESS *Tasks* ● ● ●

EFFORT →

Notes

Action Priority Matrix

TASK #	PRIORITY LIST	DUE DATE	DONE
			☐
			☐
			☐
			☐
			☐
			☐
			☐
			☐
			☐

IMPACT

QUICK *Wins* ● ● ●	MAJOR *Projects* ● ● ●
FILL-IN *Jobs* ● ● ●	THANKLESS *Tasks* ● ● ●

EFFORT

Notes

Action Priority Matrix

TASK #	PRIORITY LIST	DUE DATE	DONE
			☐
			☐
			☐
			☐
			☐
			☐
			☐
			☐
			☐

IMPACT

QUICK *Wins* ● ● ●

MAJOR *Projects* ● ● ●

FILL-IN *Jobs* ● ● ●

THANKLESS *Tasks* ● ● ●

EFFORT

Notes

Action Priority Matrix

TASK #	PRIORITY LIST	DUE DATE	DONE
			☐
			☐
			☐
			☐
			☐
			☐
			☐
			☐
			☐

IMPACT

QUICK *Wins* ● ● ●

MAJOR *Projects* ● ● ●

FILL-IN *Jobs* ● ● ●

THANKLESS *Tasks* ● ● ●

EFFORT

Notes

Action Priority Matrix

TASK #	PRIORITY LIST	DUE DATE	DONE
			☐
			☐
			☐
			☐
			☐
			☐
			☐
			☐
			☐

IMPACT

QUICK *Wins* ● ● ●

MAJOR *Projects* ● ● ●

FILL-IN *Jobs* ● ● ●

THANKLESS *Tasks* ● ● ●

EFFORT

Notes

Action Priority Matrix

TASK #	PRIORITY LIST	DUE DATE	DONE
			☐
			☐
			☐
			☐
			☐
			☐
			☐
			☐
			☐

IMPACT

QUICK *Wins* ● ● ●

MAJOR *Projects* ● ● ●

FILL-IN *Jobs* ● ● ●

THANKLESS *Tasks* ● ● ●

EFFORT

Notes

Action Priority Matrix

TASK #	PRIORITY LIST	DUE DATE	DONE
			☐
			☐
			☐
			☐
			☐
			☐
			☐
			☐
			☐

IMPACT

QUICK *Wins* ● ● ●

MAJOR *Projects* ● ● ●

FILL-IN *Jobs* ● ● ●

THANKLESS *Tasks* ● ● ●

EFFORT

Notes

Action Priority Matrix

TASK #	PRIORITY LIST	DUE DATE	DONE
			☐
			☐
			☐
			☐
			☐
			☐
			☐
			☐
			☐
			☐

IMPACT

QUICK *Wins* ● ● ●

MAJOR *Projects* ● ● ●

FILL-IN *Jobs* ● ● ●

THANKLESS *Tasks* ● ● ●

EFFORT

Notes

Action Priority Matrix

TASK #	PRIORITY LIST	DUE DATE	DONE
			☐
			☐
			☐
			☐
			☐
			☐
			☐
			☐
			☐
			☐

IMPACT

QUICK *Wins* ● ● ●	MAJOR *Projects* ● ● ●
FILL—IN *Jobs* ● ● ●	THANKLESS *Tasks* ● ● ●

EFFORT

Notes

Action Priority Matrix

TASK #	PRIORITY LIST	DUE DATE	DONE
			☐
			☐
			☐
			☐
			☐
			☐
			☐
			☐
			☐

IMPACT

QUICK *Wins* ● ● ●	MAJOR *Projects* ● ● ●
FILL-IN *Jobs* ● ● ●	THANKLESS *Tasks* ● ● ●

EFFORT

Notes

Action Priority Matrix

TASK #	PRIORITY LIST	DUE DATE	DONE
			☐
			☐
			☐
			☐
			☐
			☐
			☐
			☐
			☐

IMPACT

QUICK *Wins* ● ● ●

MAJOR *Projects* ● ● ●

FILL-IN *Jobs* ● ● ●

THANKLESS *Tasks* ● ● ●

EFFORT

Notes

Action Priority Matrix

TASK #	PRIORITY LIST	DUE DATE	DONE
			☐
			☐
			☐
			☐
			☐
			☐
			☐
			☐
			☐

IMPACT

QUICK *Wins* ● ● ●

MAJOR *Projects* ● ● ●

FILL-IN *Jobs* ● ● ●

THANKLESS *Tasks* ● ● ●

EFFORT

Notes

Action Priority Matrix

TASK #	PRIORITY LIST	DUE DATE	DONE
			☐
			☐
			☐
			☐
			☐
			☐
			☐
			☐
			☐

IMPACT

QUICK *Wins* ● ● ●

MAJOR *Projects* ● ● ●

FILL-IN *Jobs* ● ● ●

THANKLESS *Tasks* ● ● ●

EFFORT

Notes

Action Priority Matrix

TASK #	PRIORITY LIST	DUE DATE	DONE
			☐
			☐
			☐
			☐
			☐
			☐
			☐
			☐
			☐

IMPACT

QUICK *Wins* ● ● ●

MAJOR *Projects* ● ● ●

FILL-IN *Jobs* ● ● ●

THANKLESS *Tasks* ● ● ●

EFFORT

Notes

Action Priority Matrix

TASK #	PRIORITY LIST	DUE DATE	DONE
			☐
			☐
			☐
			☐
			☐
			☐
			☐
			☐
			☐

IMPACT

QUICK *Wins* ● ● ●

MAJOR *Projects* ● ● ●

FILL-IN *Jobs* ● ● ●

THANKLESS *Tasks* ● ● ●

EFFORT

Notes

Action Priority Matrix

TASK #	PRIORITY LIST	DUE DATE	DONE
			☐
			☐
			☐
			☐
			☐
			☐
			☐
			☐
			☐

IMPACT

QUICK *Wins* ● ● ●

MAJOR *Projects* ● ● ●

FILL-IN *Jobs* ● ● ●

THANKLESS *Tasks* ● ● ●

EFFORT

Notes

Action Priority Matrix

TASK #	PRIORITY LIST	DUE DATE	DONE
			☐
			☐
			☐
			☐
			☐
			☐
			☐
			☐
			☐

IMPACT

QUICK *Wins* ● ● ●

MAJOR *Projects* ● ● ●

FILL-IN *Jobs* ● ● ●

THANKLESS *Tasks* ● ● ●

EFFORT

Notes

Action Priority Matrix

TASK #	PRIORITY LIST	DUE DATE	DONE
			☐
			☐
			☐
			☐
			☐
			☐
			☐
			☐
			☐

IMPACT

QUICK *Wins* ● ● ●	MAJOR *Projects* ● ● ●
FILL-IN *Jobs* ● ● ●	THANKLESS *Tasks* ● ● ●

EFFORT

Notes

Action Priority Matrix

TASK #	PRIORITY LIST	DUE DATE	DONE
			☐
			☐
			☐
			☐
			☐
			☐
			☐
			☐
			☐
			☐

IMPACT

QUICK *Wins* ● ● ●

MAJOR *Projects* ● ● ●

FILL-IN *Jobs* ● ● ●

THANKLESS *Tasks* ● ● ●

EFFORT

Notes

Action Priority Matrix

TASK #	PRIORITY LIST	DUE DATE	DONE
			☐
			☐
			☐
			☐
			☐
			☐
			☐
			☐
			☐
			☐

IMPACT

QUICK *Wins* ● ● ●

MAJOR *Projects* ● ● ●

FILL-IN *Jobs* ● ● ●

THANKLESS *Tasks* ● ● ●

EFFORT

Notes

Action Priority Matrix

TASK #	PRIORITY LIST	DUE DATE	DONE
			☐
			☐
			☐
			☐
			☐
			☐
			☐
			☐
			☐

IMPACT

QUICK *Wins* ● ● ●

MAJOR *Projects* ● ● ●

FILL-IN *Jobs* ● ● ●

THANKLESS *Tasks* ● ● ●

EFFORT

Notes

Action Priority Matrix

TASK #	PRIORITY LIST	DUE DATE	DONE
			☐
			☐
			☐
			☐
			☐
			☐
			☐
			☐
			☐

QUICK *Wins* ● ● ●

MAJOR *Projects* ● ● ●

FILL-IN *Jobs* ● ● ●

THANKLESS *Tasks* ● ● ●

IMPACT

EFFORT

Notes

Action Priority Matrix

TASK #	PRIORITY LIST	DUE DATE	DONE
			☐
			☐
			☐
			☐
			☐
			☐
			☐
			☐
			☐

IMPACT

QUICK *Wins* ● ● ●

MAJOR *Projects* ● ● ●

FILL-IN *Jobs* ● ● ●

THANKLESS *Tasks* ● ● ●

EFFORT

Notes

Action Priority Matrix

TASK #	PRIORITY LIST	DUE DATE	DONE
			☐
			☐
			☐
			☐
			☐
			☐
			☐
			☐
			☐

IMPACT

QUICK *Wins* ● ● ●

MAJOR *Projects* ● ● ●

FILL-IN *Jobs* ● ● ●

THANKLESS *Tasks* ● ● ●

EFFORT

Notes

Action Priority Matrix

TASK #	PRIORITY LIST	DUE DATE	DONE
			☐
			☐
			☐
			☐
			☐
			☐
			☐
			☐
			☐

IMPACT

QUICK *Wins* ● ● ●	MAJOR *Projects* ● ● ●
FILL-IN *Jobs* ● ● ●	THANKLESS *Tasks* ● ● ●

EFFORT

Notes

Action Priority Matrix

TASK #	PRIORITY LIST	DUE DATE	DONE
			☐
			☐
			☐
			☐
			☐
			☐
			☐
			☐
			☐

IMPACT

QUICK *Wins* ● ● ●

MAJOR *Projects* ● ● ●

FILL-IN *Jobs* ● ● ●

THANKLESS *Tasks* ● ● ●

EFFORT

Notes

Action Priority Matrix

TASK #	PRIORITY LIST	DUE DATE	DONE
			☐
			☐
			☐
			☐
			☐
			☐
			☐
			☐
			☐

IMPACT

QUICK *Wins* ● ● ●

MAJOR *Projects* ● ● ●

FILL-IN *Jobs* ● ● ●

THANKLESS *Tasks* ● ● ●

EFFORT

Notes

Action Priority Matrix

TASK #	PRIORITY LIST	DUE DATE	DONE
			☐
			☐
			☐
			☐
			☐
			☐
			☐
			☐
			☐

IMPACT

QUICK *Wins* ● ● ●

MAJOR *Projects* ● ● ●

FILL-IN *Jobs* ● ● ●

THANKLESS *Tasks* ● ● ●

EFFORT

Notes

Action Priority Matrix

TASK #	PRIORITY LIST	DUE DATE	DONE
			☐
			☐
			☐
			☐
			☐
			☐
			☐
			☐
			☐

QUICK *Wins* ● ● ●

MAJOR *Projects* ● ● ●

FILL-IN *Jobs* ● ● ●

THANKLESS *Tasks* ● ● ●

IMPACT

EFFORT

Notes

Action Priority Matrix

TASK #	PRIORITY LIST	DUE DATE	DONE
			☐
			☐
			☐
			☐
			☐
			☐
			☐
			☐
			☐
			☐

IMPACT

QUICK *Wins* ● ● ●

MAJOR *Projects* ● ● ●

FILL-IN *Jobs* ● ● ●

THANKLESS *Tasks* ● ● ●

EFFORT

Notes

Action Priority Matrix

TASK #	PRIORITY LIST	DUE DATE	DONE
			☐
			☐
			☐
			☐
			☐
			☐
			☐
			☐
			☐

IMPACT

QUICK *Wins* ● ● ●	MAJOR *Projects* ● ● ●
FILL-IN *Jobs* ● ● ●	THANKLESS *Tasks* ● ● ●

EFFORT

Notes

Action Priority Matrix

TASK #	PRIORITY LIST	DUE DATE	DONE
			☐
			☐
			☐
			☐
			☐
			☐
			☐
			☐
			☐

IMPACT

QUICK *Wins* ● ● ●

MAJOR *Projects* ● ● ●

FILL-IN *Jobs* ● ● ●

THANKLESS *Tasks* ● ● ●

EFFORT

Notes

Action Priority Matrix

TASK #	PRIORITY LIST	DUE DATE	DONE
			☐
			☐
			☐
			☐
			☐
			☐
			☐
			☐
			☐

IMPACT

QUICK *Wins* ●●●

MAJOR *Projects* ●●●

FILL-IN *Jobs* ●●●

THANKLESS *Tasks* ●●●

EFFORT

Notes

Action Priority Matrix

TASK #	PRIORITY LIST	DUE DATE	DONE
			☐
			☐
			☐
			☐
			☐
			☐
			☐
			☐
			☐

IMPACT

QUICK *Wins* ● ● ●

MAJOR *Projects* ● ● ●

FILL-IN *Jobs* ● ● ●

THANKLESS *Tasks* ● ● ●

EFFORT

Notes

Action Priority Matrix

TASK #	PRIORITY LIST	DUE DATE	DONE
			☐
			☐
			☐
			☐
			☐
			☐
			☐
			☐
			☐

IMPACT

QUICK *Wins* ● ● ●

MAJOR *Projects* ● ● ●

FILL-IN *Jobs* ● ● ●

THANKLESS *Tasks* ● ● ●

EFFORT

Notes

Action Priority Matrix

TASK #	PRIORITY LIST	DUE DATE	DONE
			☐
			☐
			☐
			☐
			☐
			☐
			☐
			☐
			☐
			☐

IMPACT

QUICK *Wins* ● ● ●

MAJOR *Projects* ● ● ●

FILL-IN *Jobs* ● ● ●

THANKLESS *Tasks* ● ● ●

EFFORT

Notes

Action Priority Matrix

TASK #	PRIORITY LIST	DUE DATE	DONE
			☐
			☐
			☐
			☐
			☐
			☐
			☐
			☐
			☐

IMPACT

QUICK *Wins* ●●●	MAJOR *Projects* ●●●
FILL-IN *Jobs* ●●●	THANKLESS *Tasks* ●●●

EFFORT

Notes

Action Priority Matrix

TASK #	PRIORITY LIST	DUE DATE	DONE
			☐
			☐
			☐
			☐
			☐
			☐
			☐
			☐
			☐
			☐

IMPACT

QUICK *Wins* ● ● ●	MAJOR *Projects* ● ● ●
FILL-IN *Jobs* ● ● ●	THANKLESS *Tasks* ● ● ●

EFFORT

Notes

Action Priority Matrix

TASK #	PRIORITY LIST	DUE DATE	DONE
			☐
			☐
			☐
			☐
			☐
			☐
			☐
			☐
			☐

IMPACT

QUICK *Wins* ● ● ●

MAJOR *Projects* ● ● ●

FILL-IN *Jobs* ● ● ●

THANKLESS *Tasks* ● ● ●

EFFORT

Notes

Action Priority Matrix

TASK #	PRIORITY LIST	DUE DATE	DONE
			☐
			☐
			☐
			☐
			☐
			☐
			☐
			☐
			☐

IMPACT

QUICK *Wins* ● ● ●

MAJOR *Projects* ● ● ●

FILL-IN *Jobs* ● ● ●

THANKLESS *Tasks* ● ● ●

EFFORT

Notes

Action Priority Matrix

TASK #	PRIORITY LIST	DUE DATE	DONE
			☐
			☐
			☐
			☐
			☐
			☐
			☐
			☐
			☐

IMPACT

QUICK *Wins* ● ● ●

MAJOR *Projects* ● ● ●

FILL-IN *Jobs* ● ● ●

THANKLESS *Tasks* ● ● ●

EFFORT

Notes

Action Priority Matrix

TASK #	PRIORITY LIST	DUE DATE	DONE
			☐
			☐
			☐
			☐
			☐
			☐
			☐
			☐
			☐

IMPACT

QUICK *Wins* ● ● ●

MAJOR *Projects* ● ● ●

FILL-IN *Jobs* ● ● ●

THANKLESS *Tasks* ● ● ●

EFFORT

Notes

Action Priority Matrix

TASK #	PRIORITY LIST	DUE DATE	DONE
			☐
			☐
			☐
			☐
			☐
			☐
			☐
			☐
			☐

IMPACT

QUICK *Wins* ● ● ●

MAJOR *Projects* ● ● ●

FILL-IN *Jobs* ● ● ●

THANKLESS *Tasks* ● ● ●

EFFORT

Notes

Action Priority Matrix

TASK #	PRIORITY LIST	DUE DATE	DONE
			☐
			☐
			☐
			☐
			☐
			☐
			☐
			☐
			☐

QUICK *Wins* ● ● ●

MAJOR *Projects* ● ● ●

FILL-IN *Jobs* ● ● ●

THANKLESS *Tasks* ● ● ●

IMPACT

EFFORT

Notes

Action Priority Matrix

TASK #	PRIORITY LIST	DUE DATE	DONE
			☐
			☐
			☐
			☐
			☐
			☐
			☐
			☐
			☐

IMPACT

QUICK *Wins* ● ● ●

MAJOR *Projects* ● ● ●

FILL–IN *Jobs* ● ● ●

THANKLESS *Tasks* ● ● ●

EFFORT

Notes

Action Priority Matrix

TASK #	PRIORITY LIST	DUE DATE	DONE
			☐
			☐
			☐
			☐
			☐
			☐
			☐
			☐
			☐

IMPACT

QUICK *Wins* ● ● ●

MAJOR *Projects* ● ● ●

FILL-IN *Jobs* ● ● ●

THANKLESS *Tasks* ● ● ●

EFFORT

Notes

Action Priority Matrix

TASK #	PRIORITY LIST	DUE DATE	DONE
			☐
			☐
			☐
			☐
			☐
			☐
			☐
			☐
			☐

IMPACT

QUICK *Wins* ● ● ●

MAJOR *Projects* ● ● ●

FILL-IN *Jobs* ● ● ●

THANKLESS *Tasks* ● ● ●

EFFORT

Notes

Action Priority Matrix

TASK #	PRIORITY LIST	DUE DATE	DONE
			☐
			☐
			☐
			☐
			☐
			☐
			☐
			☐
			☐
			☐

IMPACT

QUICK *Wins* ● ● ●	MAJOR *Projects* ● ● ●
FILL-IN *Jobs* ● ● ●	THANKLESS *Tasks* ● ● ●

EFFORT

Notes

Action Priority Matrix

TASK #	PRIORITY LIST	DUE DATE	DONE
			☐
			☐
			☐
			☐
			☐
			☐
			☐
			☐
			☐

IMPACT

QUICK *Wins* ● ● ●

MAJOR *Projects* ● ● ●

FILL-IN *Jobs* ● ● ●

THANKLESS *Tasks* ● ● ●

EFFORT

Notes

Action Priority Matrix

TASK #	PRIORITY LIST	DUE DATE	DONE
			☐
			☐
			☐
			☐
			☐
			☐
			☐
			☐
			☐

IMPACT

QUICK *Wins* ● ● ●

MAJOR *Projects* ● ● ●

FILL-IN *Jobs* ● ● ●

THANKLESS *Tasks* ● ● ●

EFFORT

Notes

Action Priority Matrix

TASK #	PRIORITY LIST	DUE DATE	DONE
			☐
			☐
			☐
			☐
			☐
			☐
			☐
			☐
			☐

IMPACT

QUICK *Wins* ● ● ●

MAJOR *Projects* ● ● ●

FILL-IN *Jobs* ● ● ●

THANKLESS *Tasks* ● ● ●

EFFORT

Notes

Action Priority Matrix

TASK #	PRIORITY LIST	DUE DATE	DONE
			☐
			☐
			☐
			☐
			☐
			☐
			☐
			☐
			☐

IMPACT

QUICK *Wins* ● ● ●

MAJOR *Projects* ● ● ●

FILL-IN *Jobs* ● ● ●

THANKLESS *Tasks* ● ● ●

EFFORT

Notes

Action Priority Matrix

TASK #	PRIORITY LIST	DUE DATE	DONE
			☐
			☐
			☐
			☐
			☐
			☐
			☐
			☐
			☐

IMPACT

QUICK *Wins* ● ● ●

MAJOR *Projects* ● ● ●

FILL-IN *Jobs* ● ● ●

THANKLESS *Tasks* ● ● ●

EFFORT

Notes

Action Priority Matrix

TASK #	PRIORITY LIST	DUE DATE	DONE
			☐
			☐
			☐
			☐
			☐
			☐
			☐
			☐
			☐

IMPACT

QUICK *Wins* ● ● ●

MAJOR *Projects* ● ● ●

FILL-IN *Jobs* ● ● ●

THANKLESS *Tasks* ● ● ●

EFFORT

Notes

Action Priority Matrix

TASK #	PRIORITY LIST	DUE DATE	DONE
			☐
			☐
			☐
			☐
			☐
			☐
			☐
			☐
			☐

IMPACT

QUICK *Wins* ● ● ●	MAJOR *Projects* ● ● ●
FILL-IN *Jobs* ● ● ●	THANKLESS *Tasks* ● ● ●

EFFORT

Notes

Action Priority Matrix

TASK #	PRIORITY LIST	DUE DATE	DONE
			☐
			☐
			☐
			☐
			☐
			☐
			☐
			☐
			☐

IMPACT

QUICK *Wins* ● ● ●

MAJOR *Projects* ● ● ●

FILL-IN *Jobs* ● ● ●

THANKLESS *Tasks* ● ● ●

EFFORT

Notes

Action Priority Matrix

TASK #	PRIORITY LIST	DUE DATE	DONE
			☐
			☐
			☐
			☐
			☐
			☐
			☐
			☐
			☐

IMPACT

QUICK *Wins* ● ● ●

MAJOR *Projects* ● ● ●

FILL-IN *Jobs* ● ● ●

THANKLESS *Tasks* ● ● ●

EFFORT

Notes

Action Priority Matrix

TASK #	PRIORITY LIST	DUE DATE	DONE
			☐
			☐
			☐
			☐
			☐
			☐
			☐
			☐
			☐

IMPACT

QUICK *Wins* ● ● ●

MAJOR *Projects* ● ● ●

FILL-IN *Jobs* ● ● ●

THANKLESS *Tasks* ● ● ●

EFFORT

Notes

Action Priority Matrix

TASK #	PRIORITY LIST	DUE DATE	DONE
			☐
			☐
			☐
			☐
			☐
			☐
			☐
			☐
			☐

IMPACT

QUICK *Wins* ● ● ●	MAJOR *Projects* ● ● ●
FILL-IN *Jobs* ● ● ●	THANKLESS *Tasks* ● ● ●

EFFORT

Notes

Action Priority Matrix

TASK #	PRIORITY LIST	DUE DATE	DONE
			☐
			☐
			☐
			☐
			☐
			☐
			☐
			☐
			☐

IMPACT

QUICK *Wins* ● ● ●

MAJOR *Projects* ● ● ●

FILL-IN *Jobs* ● ● ●

THANKLESS *Tasks* ● ● ●

EFFORT

Notes

Action Priority Matrix

TASK #	PRIORITY LIST	DUE DATE	DONE
			☐
			☐
			☐
			☐
			☐
			☐
			☐
			☐
			☐

IMPACT

QUICK *Wins* ● ● ●

MAJOR *Projects* ● ● ●

FILL-IN *Jobs* ● ● ●

THANKLESS *Tasks* ● ● ●

EFFORT

Notes

Action Priority Matrix

TASK #	PRIORITY LIST	DUE DATE	DONE
			☐
			☐
			☐
			☐
			☐
			☐
			☐
			☐
			☐

IMPACT

QUICK *Wins* ● ● ●

MAJOR *Projects* ● ● ●

FILL-IN *Jobs* ● ● ●

THANKLESS *Tasks* ● ● ●

EFFORT

Notes

Action Priority Matrix

TASK #	PRIORITY LIST	DUE DATE	DONE
			☐
			☐
			☐
			☐
			☐
			☐
			☐
			☐
			☐

IMPACT

QUICK *Wins* ● ● ●

MAJOR *Projects* ● ● ●

FILL-IN *Jobs* ● ● ●

THANKLESS *Tasks* ● ● ●

EFFORT

Notes

Action Priority Matrix

TASK #	PRIORITY LIST	DUE DATE	DONE
			☐
			☐
			☐
			☐
			☐
			☐
			☐
			☐
			☐

IMPACT

QUICK *Wins* ● ● ●

MAJOR *Projects* ● ● ●

FILL-IN *Jobs* ● ● ●

THANKLESS *Tasks* ● ● ●

EFFORT

Notes

Action Priority Matrix

TASK #	PRIORITY LIST	DUE DATE	DONE
			☐
			☐
			☐
			☐
			☐
			☐
			☐
			☐
			☐

IMPACT

QUICK *Wins* ● ● ●

MAJOR *Projects* ● ● ●

FILL-IN *Jobs* ● ● ●

THANKLESS *Tasks* ● ● ●

EFFORT

Notes

Action Priority Matrix

TASK #	PRIORITY LIST	DUE DATE	DONE
			☐
			☐
			☐
			☐
			☐
			☐
			☐
			☐
			☐

IMPACT

QUICK *Wins* ● ● ●

MAJOR *Projects* ● ● ●

FILL-IN *Jobs* ● ● ●

THANKLESS *Tasks* ● ● ●

EFFORT

Notes

Action Priority Matrix

TASK #	PRIORITY LIST	DUE DATE	DONE
			☐
			☐
			☐
			☐
			☐
			☐
			☐
			☐
			☐

IMPACT

QUICK *Wins* ● ● ●

MAJOR *Projects* ● ● ●

FILL-IN *Jobs* ● ● ●

THANKLESS *Tasks* ● ● ●

EFFORT

Notes

Action Priority Matrix

TASK #	PRIORITY LIST	DUE DATE	DONE
			☐
			☐
			☐
			☐
			☐
			☐
			☐
			☐
			☐

IMPACT

QUICK *Wins* ● ● ●	MAJOR *Projects* ● ● ●
FILL-IN *Jobs* ● ● ●	THANKLESS *Tasks* ● ● ●

EFFORT

Notes

Action Priority Matrix

TASK #	PRIORITY LIST	DUE DATE	DONE
			☐
			☐
			☐
			☐
			☐
			☐
			☐
			☐
			☐

IMPACT

QUICK *Wins* ● ● ●

MAJOR *Projects* ● ● ●

FILL-IN *Jobs* ● ● ●

THANKLESS *Tasks* ● ● ●

EFFORT

Notes

Action Priority Matrix

TASK #	PRIORITY LIST	DUE DATE	DONE
			☐
			☐
			☐
			☐
			☐
			☐
			☐
			☐
			☐

IMPACT

QUICK *Wins* ● ● ●

MAJOR *Projects* ● ● ●

FILL-IN *Jobs* ● ● ●

THANKLESS *Tasks* ● ● ●

EFFORT

Notes

Action Priority Matrix

TASK #	PRIORITY LIST	DUE DATE	DONE
			☐
			☐
			☐
			☐
			☐
			☐
			☐
			☐
			☐

IMPACT

QUICK *Wins* ● ● ●

MAJOR *Projects* ● ● ●

FILL-IN *Jobs* ● ● ●

THANKLESS *Tasks* ● ● ●

EFFORT

Notes

Action Priority Matrix

TASK #	PRIORITY LIST	DUE DATE	DONE
			☐
			☐
			☐
			☐
			☐
			☐
			☐
			☐
			☐

IMPACT

QUICK *Wins* ● ● ●

MAJOR *Projects* ● ● ●

FILL-IN *Jobs* ● ● ●

THANKLESS *Tasks* ● ● ●

EFFORT

Notes

Action Priority Matrix

TASK #	PRIORITY LIST	DUE DATE	DONE
			☐
			☐
			☐
			☐
			☐
			☐
			☐
			☐
			☐

IMPACT

QUICK *Wins* ● ● ●

MAJOR *Projects* ● ● ●

FILL-IN *Jobs* ● ● ●

THANKLESS *Tasks* ● ● ●

EFFORT

Notes

Action Priority Matrix

TASK #	PRIORITY LIST	DUE DATE	DONE
			☐
			☐
			☐
			☐
			☐
			☐
			☐
			☐
			☐

IMPACT

QUICK *Wins* ● ● ●

MAJOR *Projects* ● ● ●

FILL-IN *Jobs* ● ● ●

THANKLESS *Tasks* ● ● ●

EFFORT

Notes

Action Priority Matrix

TASK #	PRIORITY LIST	DUE DATE	DONE
			☐
			☐
			☐
			☐
			☐
			☐
			☐
			☐
			☐

IMPACT

QUICK *Wins* ● ● ●

MAJOR *Projects* ● ● ●

FILL–IN *Jobs* ● ● ●

THANKLESS *Tasks* ● ● ●

EFFORT

Notes

Action Priority Matrix

TASK #	PRIORITY LIST	DUE DATE	DONE
			☐
			☐
			☐
			☐
			☐
			☐
			☐
			☐
			☐
			☐

IMPACT

QUICK *Wins* ● ● ●

MAJOR *Projects* ● ● ●

FILL-IN *Jobs* ● ● ●

THANKLESS *Tasks* ● ● ●

EFFORT

Notes

Action Priority Matrix

TASK #	PRIORITY LIST	DUE DATE	DONE
			☐
			☐
			☐
			☐
			☐
			☐
			☐
			☐
			☐

IMPACT

QUICK *Wins* ● ● ●	MAJOR *Projects* ● ● ●
FILL–IN *Jobs* ● ● ●	THANKLESS *Tasks* ● ● ●

EFFORT

Notes

Action Priority Matrix

TASK #	PRIORITY LIST	DUE DATE	DONE
			☐
			☐
			☐
			☐
			☐
			☐
			☐
			☐
			☐

IMPACT

QUICK *Wins* ● ● ●

MAJOR *Projects* ● ● ●

FILL-IN *Jobs* ● ● ●

THANKLESS *Tasks* ● ● ●

EFFORT

Notes

Action Priority Matrix

TASK #	PRIORITY LIST	DUE DATE	DONE
			☐
			☐
			☐
			☐
			☐
			☐
			☐
			☐
			☐

IMPACT

QUICK *Wins* ● ● ●

MAJOR *Projects* ● ● ●

FILL-IN *Jobs* ● ● ●

THANKLESS *Tasks* ● ● ●

EFFORT

Notes

Action Priority Matrix

TASK #	PRIORITY LIST	DUE DATE	DONE
			☐
			☐
			☐
			☐
			☐
			☐
			☐
			☐
			☐

IMPACT

QUICK *Wins* ● ● ●

MAJOR *Projects* ● ● ●

FILL-IN *Jobs* ● ● ●

THANKLESS *Tasks* ● ● ●

EFFORT

Notes

Action Priority Matrix

TASK #	PRIORITY LIST	DUE DATE	DONE
			☐
			☐
			☐
			☐
			☐
			☐
			☐
			☐
			☐

IMPACT

QUICK *Wins* ● ● ●	MAJOR *Projects* ● ● ●
FILL-IN *Jobs* ● ● ●	THANKLESS *Tasks* ● ● ●

EFFORT

Notes

Action Priority Matrix

TASK #	PRIORITY LIST	DUE DATE	DONE
			☐
			☐
			☐
			☐
			☐
			☐
			☐
			☐
			☐

IMPACT

QUICK *Wins* ● ● ●

MAJOR *Projects* ● ● ●

FILL-IN *Jobs* ● ● ●

THANKLESS *Tasks* ● ● ●

EFFORT

Notes

Action Priority Matrix

TASK #	PRIORITY LIST	DUE DATE	DONE
			☐
			☐
			☐
			☐
			☐
			☐
			☐
			☐
			☐

IMPACT

QUICK *Wins* ● ● ●

MAJOR *Projects* ● ● ●

FILL-IN *Jobs* ● ● ●

THANKLESS *Tasks* ● ● ●

EFFORT

Notes

Action Priority Matrix

TASK #	PRIORITY LIST	DUE DATE	DONE
			☐
			☐
			☐
			☐
			☐
			☐
			☐
			☐
			☐
			☐

IMPACT

QUICK *Wins* ● ● ●

MAJOR *Projects* ● ● ●

FILL-IN *Jobs* ● ● ●

THANKLESS *Tasks* ● ● ●

EFFORT

Notes

Action Priority Matrix

TASK #	PRIORITY LIST	DUE DATE	DONE
			☐
			☐
			☐
			☐
			☐
			☐
			☐
			☐
			☐

IMPACT

QUICK *Wins* ● ● ●

MAJOR *Projects* ● ● ●

FILL-IN *Jobs* ● ● ●

THANKLESS *Tasks* ● ● ●

EFFORT

Notes

Action Priority Matrix

TASK #	PRIORITY LIST	DUE DATE	DONE
			☐
			☐
			☐
			☐
			☐
			☐
			☐
			☐
			☐

IMPACT

QUICK *Wins* ● ● ●

MAJOR *Projects* ● ● ●

FILL-IN *Jobs* ● ● ●

THANKLESS *Tasks* ● ● ●

EFFORT

Notes

Action Priority Matrix

TASK #	PRIORITY LIST	DUE DATE	DONE
			☐
			☐
			☐
			☐
			☐
			☐
			☐
			☐
			☐

IMPACT

QUICK *Wins* ● ● ●

MAJOR *Projects* ● ● ●

FILL-IN *Jobs* ● ● ●

THANKLESS *Tasks* ● ● ●

EFFORT

Notes

Action Priority Matrix

TASK #	PRIORITY LIST	DUE DATE	DONE
			☐
			☐
			☐
			☐
			☐
			☐
			☐
			☐
			☐

IMPACT

QUICK *Wins* ● ● ●

MAJOR *Projects* ● ● ●

FILL-IN *Jobs* ● ● ●

THANKLESS *Tasks* ● ● ●

EFFORT

Notes

Action Priority Matrix

TASK #	PRIORITY LIST	DUE DATE	DONE
			☐
			☐
			☐
			☐
			☐
			☐
			☐
			☐
			☐

IMPACT

QUICK *Wins* ● ● ●

MAJOR *Projects* ● ● ●

FILL-IN *Jobs* ● ● ●

THANKLESS *Tasks* ● ● ●

EFFORT

Notes

Action Priority Matrix

TASK #	PRIORITY LIST	DUE DATE	DONE
			☐
			☐
			☐
			☐
			☐
			☐
			☐
			☐
			☐
			☐

IMPACT

QUICK *Wins* ● ● ●

MAJOR *Projects* ● ● ●

FILL-IN *Jobs* ● ● ●

THANKLESS *Tasks* ● ● ●

EFFORT

Notes

Action Priority Matrix

TASK #	PRIORITY LIST	DUE DATE	DONE
			☐
			☐
			☐
			☐
			☐
			☐
			☐
			☐
			☐

IMPACT →

QUICK *Wins* ● ● ●

MAJOR *Projects* ● ● ●

FILL-IN *Jobs* ● ● ●

THANKLESS *Tasks* ● ● ●

EFFORT →

Notes

Action Priority Matrix

TASK #	PRIORITY LIST	DUE DATE	DONE
			☐
			☐
			☐
			☐
			☐
			☐
			☐
			☐
			☐

IMPACT ↑

QUICK *Wins* ● ● ●	MAJOR *Projects* ● ● ●

FILL-IN *Jobs* ● ● ●	THANKLESS *Tasks* ● ● ●

EFFORT →

Notes

Action Priority Matrix

TASK #	PRIORITY LIST	DUE DATE	DONE
			☐
			☐
			☐
			☐
			☐
			☐
			☐
			☐
			☐

IMPACT

QUICK *Wins* ● ● ●	MAJOR *Projects* ● ● ●
FILL–IN *Jobs* ● ● ●	THANKLESS *Tasks* ● ● ●

EFFORT

Notes

Action Priority Matrix

TASK #	PRIORITY LIST	DUE DATE	DONE
			☐
			☐
			☐
			☐
			☐
			☐
			☐
			☐
			☐

IMPACT

QUICK *Wins* ● ● ●

MAJOR *Projects* ● ● ●

FILL-IN *Jobs* ● ● ●

THANKLESS *Tasks* ● ● ●

EFFORT

Notes

Action Priority Matrix

TASK #	PRIORITY LIST	DUE DATE	DONE
			☐
			☐
			☐
			☐
			☐
			☐
			☐
			☐
			☐

IMPACT

QUICK *Wins* ● ● ●

MAJOR *Projects* ● ● ●

FILL-IN *Jobs* ● ● ●

THANKLESS *Tasks* ● ● ●

EFFORT

Notes

Action Priority Matrix

TASK #	PRIORITY LIST	DUE DATE	DONE
			☐
			☐
			☐
			☐
			☐
			☐
			☐
			☐
			☐

IMPACT

QUICK *Wins* ● ● ●

MAJOR *Projects* ● ● ●

FILL-IN *Jobs* ● ● ●

THANKLESS *Tasks* ● ● ●

EFFORT

Notes

Action Priority Matrix

TASK #	PRIORITY LIST	DUE DATE	DONE
			☐
			☐
			☐
			☐
			☐
			☐
			☐
			☐
			☐

IMPACT

QUICK *Wins* ● ● ●

MAJOR *Projects* ● ● ●

FILL-IN *Jobs* ● ● ●

THANKLESS *Tasks* ● ● ●

EFFORT

Notes

Action Priority Matrix

TASK #	PRIORITY LIST	DUE DATE	DONE
			☐
			☐
			☐
			☐
			☐
			☐
			☐
			☐
			☐

QUICK *Wins* ● ● ●

MAJOR *Projects* ● ● ●

FILL-IN *Jobs* ● ● ●

THANKLESS *Tasks* ● ● ●

IMPACT

EFFORT

Notes

Action Priority Matrix

TASK #	PRIORITY LIST	DUE DATE	DONE
			☐
			☐
			☐
			☐
			☐
			☐
			☐
			☐
			☐

IMPACT

QUICK *Wins* ● ● ●

MAJOR *Projects* ● ● ●

FILL-IN *Jobs* ● ● ●

THANKLESS *Tasks* ● ● ●

EFFORT

Notes

Action Priority Matrix

TASK #	PRIORITY LIST	DUE DATE	DONE
			☐
			☐
			☐
			☐
			☐
			☐
			☐
			☐
			☐

IMPACT

QUICK *Wins* ● ● ●

MAJOR *Projects* ● ● ●

FILL-IN *Jobs* ● ● ●

THANKLESS *Tasks* ● ● ●

EFFORT

Notes

Made in the USA
Las Vegas, NV
18 February 2021